Shigeru Miyamoto

Nintendo Game Designer

Other titles in the Innovators series include:

INNOVATORS

Shigeru Miyamoto
Nintendo Game Designer

JAN BURNS

KIDHAVEN PRESS

An imprint of Thomson Gale, a part of The Thomson Corporation

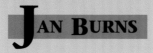

THOMSON

★

GALE

™

Detroit • New York • San Francisco • San Diego • New Haven, Conn. • Waterville, Maine • London • Munich

LIBRARY OF CONGRESS CATALOGING-IN-PUBLICATION DATA

Burns, Jan.
  Shigeru Miyamoto / by Jan Burns.
    p. cm. -- (Inventors and creators)
  Includes bibliographical references and index.
  ISBN 0-7377-3534-1 (hard cover : alk. paper) 1. Computer games—Programming—Juvenile literature. 2. Video games—Design—Juvenile literature. 3. Miyamoto, Shigeru, 1952—Juvenile literature. I. Title. II. Series.
  QA76.76.C672B865 2006
  794.8'1526--dc22   2005030258

Printed in the United States of America

CONTENTS

INTRODUCTION

Legendary Video Game Designer

Shigeru Miyamoto is the most successful **video game** designer in the world. Millions of players eagerly reserve his games months before they hit the stores. Many of his groundbreaking, imaginative games, such as *Donkey Kong, Super Mario Bros.,* and *The Legend of Zelda,* have become global classics and huge moneymakers. Within these games his remarkable characters Mario, Donkey Kong, Zelda, Link, and others have delighted and intrigued people for years.

Miyamoto has won numerous awards in recognition of his work, two of which are especially notable. In 1998 he was the first person ever to be inducted into the Academy of Interactive Arts and Sciences (AIAS) Hall of Fame. The award was given in recognition of his lifetime achievement and dramatic effect on the video game industry. In 2005 he was among the first honorees to receive a star on the Walk of Game, a section of San Francisco's Metreon Center that is modeled after Hollywood's Walk of Fame. Despite his achievements, Miyamoto is extremely modest about

Shigeru Miyamoto is considered a creative genius in the world of video games.

his success. When someone tells him that he is a genius, he laughs and changes the subject. But there is no denying that he is one of the world's greatest pioneers in video game design.

CHAPTER 1

A Creative Mind

Shigeru Miyamoto was born on November 16, 1952. He grew up in the countryside near Kyoto, Japan, in the town of Sonobe. He and his family lived in a small house made from paper and cedar wood. Sliding screens, rather than doors, separated the rooms. A rice field sat just beyond. After the yearly harvest, when the field had dried out, it was used as a park. Miyamoto played baseball there with other children.

Miyamoto's parents did not own a television, so he and his family had to find other ways to keep busy. For entertainment, his family would travel to Kyoto by train to shop and see movies, such as *Peter Pan* and *Snow White*. Back at home, Miyamoto enjoyed reading science fiction stories by Isaac Asimov, and detective stories by Sir Arthur Conan Doyle, the creator of Sherlock Holmes. Miyamoto especially liked to play in his parents' attic with his friends. The boys used the attic as a kind of clubhouse or meeting place. There they had fun developing secret codes and passwords.

Fascination with Nature

Miyamoto also found pleasure in the natural world. He loved to hike around the countryside surrounding his home. He explored the banks of rice fields, canyons, grassy hills, and waterways and then made sketches of these places.

The young artist was a careful observer. He noted the details of his surroundings. He saw the way the water glistened in creeks, the uneven texture of a grassy hillside, and the outlines of the cliffs around a canyon.

One day Miyamoto discovered a large hole in the ground alongside a hill. He returned to it several times before he gathered enough courage to enter it. He discovered that the hole was really

As a youth, Shigeru Miyamoto was fascinated by the hidden, underground caverns near his home.

the mouth of a cave. With a homemade lantern, he explored the cave and found another hole that led to a deeper cavern. He returned to the cave again and again, venturing farther in each time, and exploring it a bit more each trip. He was fascinated by his discovery, and proud that he had dared to enter the hole.

Miyamoto later stated that he never forgot the excitement of finding the cave inside the hole, saying, "What if you walk along and everything that you see is more than what you see—the person in the t-shirt and slacks is a warrior, the space that appears empty is a secret door to an alternate world?"[1]

Cartooning

More than anything Miyamoto liked to draw cartoons. He created all kinds of lively characters. He spent much of his free time practicing his drawing, and he became skilled at drawing characters that showed a wide range of emotions through their facial expressions and body language. Miyamoto was a perfectionist, constantly trying to improve the look of the characters he designed. He filled entire sketchbooks with these drawings.

Sometimes Miyamoto created cartoon flip-books. He drew a cartoon character on one page of a notebook, and on each of the succeeding pages drew the character again and again. In each new picture, he made small changes to the character's face, body, and the position of its arms and legs. If he flipped through the pages quickly, the character looked as if it were moving.

Career Choice

Miyamoto wanted to learn more about art, so in 1970 he entered the Kanazawa College of Art. His love of drawing continued to flourish, and he often sketched happily for hours. Although he sometimes skipped classes so he could have more time to draw,

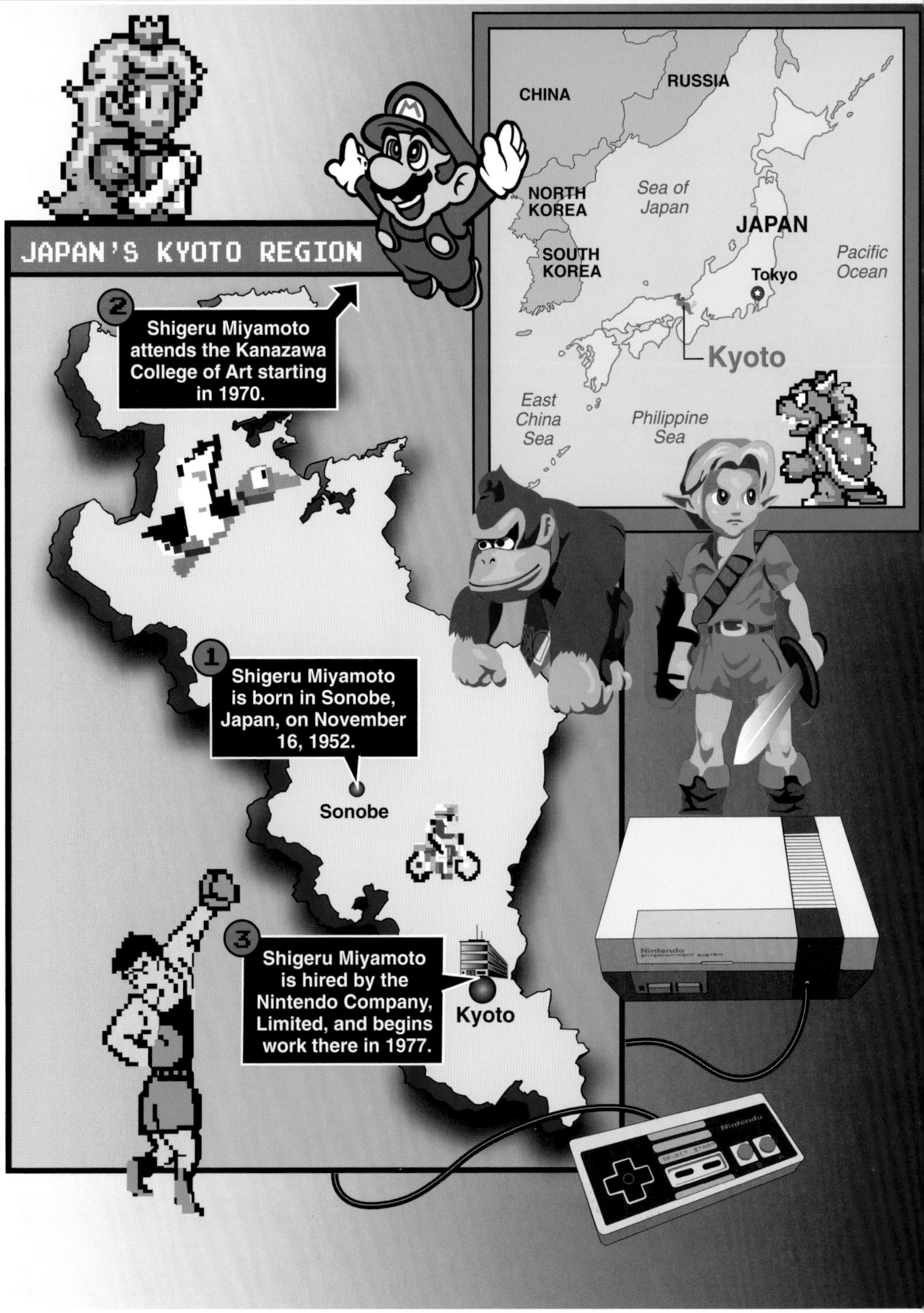

JAPAN'S KYOTO REGION

CHINA **RUSSIA**

NORTH KOREA

Sea of Japan

JAPAN

SOUTH KOREA

Tokyo

Pacific Ocean

Kyoto

East China Sea

Philippine Sea

② Shigeru Miyamoto attends the Kanazawa College of Art starting in 1970.

① Shigeru Miyamoto is born in Sonobe, Japan, on November 16, 1952.

Sonobe

③ Shigeru Miyamoto is hired by the Nintendo Company, Limited, and begins work there in 1977.

Kyoto

he persisted with school, and after five years he graduated with a degree in industrial design.

After Miyamoto graduated, he took some time to think about what type of career would satisfy him. He wanted to do something creative. He considered being a puppeteer or a painter and then decided he might like to design toys. Miyamoto finally asked his father to contact one of his old school friends, Hiroshi Yamauchi, who ran a toy and playing-card company called Nintendo Company, Limited, and ask that a job interview be set up for him.

Job Interview

When the two men met in 1977, Yamauchi told Miyamoto, "We need engineers, not painters."[2] However, he liked the 24-year-old, with his shaggy hair, wide smile, and enthusiastic way of talking. He asked Miyamoto to develop some product ideas for children and bring them back to him. Miyamoto agreed.

At the next meeting, Miyamoto presented Yamauchi with some sketches and a brightly painted clothes hanger that he had designed for children. He explained that the sharp point of most

traditional wire hangers was potentially dangerous to small children. His hanger was carved out of soft wood, into the shape of the head of an elephant. Children could hang clothes over the big ears and curved trunk. The head itself could easily be attached to any door or wall.

Hiroshi Yamauchi gave Miyamoto his first big break.

Yamauchi was a shrewd businessman, and an excellent judge of character. He was impressed by Miyamoto's ingenuity and resourcefulness. He hired him to become Nintendo's first staff artist, to create artwork for toys. Nintendo did not even need a full-time artist at the time, but Yamauchi believed that Miyamoto was extremely talented, and he wanted him to become part of his company.

First Challenge at Nintendo

Over the next few years Yamauchi decided that he wanted Nintendo to expand. He thought a good way to do this was to get into the business of producing coin-operated **arcade games** in the United States. He believed it could bring in to his company a large amount of money that would pay for the expansion.

He directed his son-in-law Minoru Arakawa, who was the president of Nintendo of America (NOA), to find a game that would appeal to American children. Arakawa selected an arcade game that had done fairly well in Japan and had been successful at test locations in Seattle, Washington. *Radarscope* was a simple shooting game, where players had to shoot down enemy fighters. He ordered 3,000 units, hoping that it would become a best seller, but arcade owners bought only 1,000 of the machines. The company needed a different game.

Nintendo's best programmers and engineers were already working on other important projects. As a result, in 1980 Yamauchi called Miyamoto into his office and told him about the failure of the *Radarscope* game, and asked him to design a coin-operated arcade game that Nintendo could sell in the United States.

Miyamoto realized that this was his chance to advance his career at Nintendo. Up until then he had been designing characters for arcade games and making the posters that went on the outside

One of Miyamoto's first big projects was designing coin-operated arcade games like these.

of arcade game units. He did not know how to create or program an arcade game. He would have to learn new skills and the work would be challenging, but it was an opportunity that he could not pass up. After careful consideration he accepted Yamauchi's offer, knowing that the outcome could change his life.

CHAPTER 2

Early Success

When Miyamoto was put in charge of the new project to design a coin-operated arcade game that Nintendo could sell in the United States, it caused considerable surprise among Nintendo employees. He said some of them asked, "What can this long-haired student do? Who is this guy?"[3] Miyamoto heard the comments, but he ignored them. He enjoyed challenges and felt that he could succeed.

Creating an Action Game

Miyamoto wanted to develop something totally different from the simple shooting games that filled the arcades at that time. So he decided to create a game of continuous action, where players could advance to different levels of the game. His game would also be one of the first to have characters and a story line.

He wanted his main character to be able to jump, so his game would be the first arcade game to have a **jump button**, a button that players can push to make a character jump into the air. Because of

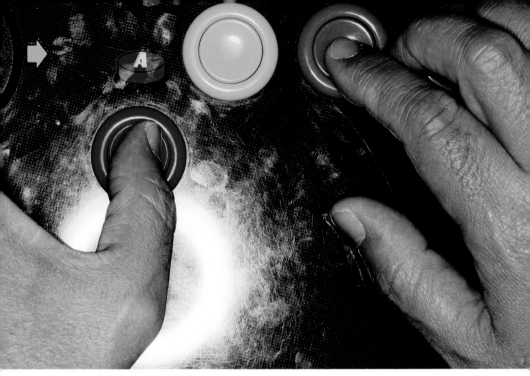

In Miyamoto's first game, players pushed buttons
to make the characters move.

his jumping ability, Miyamoto decided to name his main character
Jumpman.

Donkey Kong

In the game, an angry gorilla escapes from his master (Jumpman), kidnaps his master's girlfriend, a beautiful girl named
Pauline, and takes her to the top of a construction site. Players
have to guide Jumpman to the top of the building, so he can rescue Pauline. To succeed, Jumpman has to run up ramps, climb
ladders, and jump on platforms and elevators, all the while dodg-
ing the barrels, fireballs, and bouncing rivets that the gorilla is
tossing down at him.

Miyamoto wanted his main character, Jumpman, to be a person that the game's players would like and identify with. So he
made him a hardworking, ordinary person who was a bit goofy

and awkward. After much thought, he designed Jumpman as a pudgy carpenter with a huge nose. He purposely made Jumpman short, because he wanted him to be smaller than any enemy characters he fought against. He thought this would make their fight even more impressive when Jumpman won.

The game would be named after the enemy gorilla, Donkey Kong. He thought up the Kong part of the name from the giant gorilla that was in the movie *King Kong*. But, according to Miyamoto, his gorilla "would not be too evil or repulsive."[4] For the first part of the name he wanted a word like stubborn, so he chose the word donkey.

Technical Matters

Miyamoto had no computer programming experience, so he met with Gunpei Yokoi, head of one of Nintendo's three research and development teams, as well as programmers at the company to

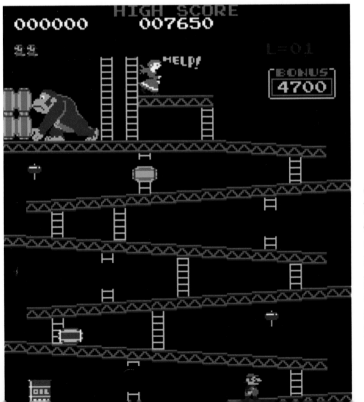

One of Miyamoto's earliest characters, Donkey Kong prepares to drop barrels that will block Mario's climb.

17

discuss technical issues. He wanted to know how big the characters should be, how to make them stand out on a small arcade screen, and what types of movements they could make.

The engineers informed Miyamoto that they had only a limited number of available colors and **pixels**, tiny dots that make up a picture in a computer's memory, available to them. Because of the limited technology and few colors that they could use, Miyamoto designed Jumpman wearing bright red overalls to make him easily visible. He also drew him with a big mustache instead of a mouth, and gave him a hat instead of hair because both showed up well on the screen.

Mario Joins the Game

By late 1981 Miyamoto had completed *Donkey Kong*. Before it was released, Nintendo executive Arakawa decided to rename Jumpman. After looking at the chubby carpenter's face, he decided it looked exactly like the landlord of Nintendo's Seattle, Washington, warehouse, Mario Segali. So Jumpman became Mario.

Donkey Kong succeeded beyond anyone's expectations. It was fun to play and offered a totally different type of entertainment. It became Nintendo's first real smash hit and was one of the most successful arcade games ever released. The demand was so great for the game that Miyamoto developed the **sequels** *Donkey Kong Jr.* and *Donkey Kong 3*. These, too, sold very well.

"The decision (to challenge Miyamoto to make a game) was one of the smartest Nintendo president Hiroshi Yamauchi would ever make. Miyamoto, it was soon apparent, had the same talent for video games as the Beatles had for popular music,"[5] according to David Sheff, in his book *Game Over*.

In 1983 Miyamoto let Mario star in his own game, which he called *Mario Bros*. A coworker had suggested that Mario looked

Miyamoto poses with a life-size Mario, one of his most popular characters.

more like a plumber than a carpenter. Miyamoto agreed, and in this game, plumber Mario and his brother Luigi have to clear underground sewer pipes of unwanted pests, such as crabs, turtles, and fireflies. Again, Miyamoto's game was a big seller.

More Challenges and Responsibility

Yamauchi was impressed with Miyamoto's success. He saw how much Miyamoto had learned over the years, so in 1984 he gave him his own development team. It was called the Research & Development 4 team.

Yamauchi wanted to expand Nintendo's business into the home video game market, and was getting ready to **launch** the Nintendo Entertainment System (NES) in the United States. He believed that more people would buy the game-playing machine if there was a great game ready to sell with it. He hoped that Miyamoto and his team could accomplish this goal.

Super Mario Bros.

In response, Miyamoto created *Super Mario Bros.,* which was released in 1985, for the NES. It was the first game where the playing field **scrolled**, or moved across the screen, instead of having all the action confined to a single screen. In the game Mario and his brother Luigi have to defeat archrival Bowser, King of the Koopas, and rescue Princess Peach Toadstool.

The inventor demonstrates a popular Mario game on a Nintendo system.

To rescue the princess, Mario must travel through eight challenging worlds. Each world is packed with puzzles that Mario has to unravel and monsters that he must defeat. The game encourages players to find secret areas within the levels by rewarding them when they find one.

Super Mario Bros. takes place in the colorful world of the Mushroom Kingdom, where life is absurd or crazy. Mushrooms make Mario grow taller, flowers enable him to shoot fireballs, and Warpzones allow him to skip over levels.

"I think great video games are like favorite playgrounds, places you become attached to and go back to again and again. Wouldn't it be great to have a whole drawer full of 'playgrounds' right at your fingertips?"[6] Miyamoto asked.

What Inspires Him

In designing *Super Mario Bros.,* Miyamoto found inspiration from favorite shows and books and even his childhood. He said that the Warpzones were inspired by seeing warp speed, which is extremely fast speed, used in the science fiction television series *Star Trek.* Reading the book *Alice's Adventures in Wonderland* gave him the idea to use mushrooms as **power-ups**. (In the book, Alice eats and drinks various substances to make her either taller or smaller.) Memories of exploring caves when he was young inspired Miyamoto to create the underground levels in the game, and his memory of his parents' attic, which he used with his friends as a meeting place, gave him the idea to design the safe places in the game.

Super Mario Bros. revolutionized the games industry, with its side-scrolling, power-ups, extra lives given as rewards to allow players to play longer, and hidden areas. The game's success changed many people's earlier assumptions that video games

Miyamoto's ideas for Super Mario Bros. came from many places, including Lewis Carroll's _Alice's Adventures in Wonderland_.

were just a fad, because they were now part of a highly successful industry worth millions of dollars. Many in the video game industry wondered what Shigeru Miyamoto would come up with next.

CHAPTER 3

Nintendo's Shining Star

After the *Super Mario Bros.* game was released, Miyamoto's duties expanded so that he had to develop a number of games at the same time, instead of only one. This required dedication, focus, and often working late into the night.

The Legend of Zelda

The Legend of Zelda, released in 1987, was an **adventure/ role-playing game (RPG)** that Miyamoto developed over a three-year period with a team of 140 people. In RPG games, players do not just watch characters in games. The games are designed so players feel they actually are one of the characters. Miyamoto later stated that this was the most difficult game he had ever produced.

Players assume the role of a young elf named Link as he travels through the sprawling fantasyland of Hyrule to rescue Princess Zelda. In contrast to Mario's humorous appearance, Link is slender and carries a shield and a bow, with a quiver of arrows over one shoulder. He has pointed ears and is clad in green and brown, for camouflage.

In the game, Link has to battle everything from bats to dragons, while exploring a series of dungeons, shadowy forests, oceans, creepy graveyards, hidden caves, and temples. It is such a challenging game that players get an incredible feeling of accomplishment when they finally rescue Zelda.

During a press briefing, Miyamoto imitates his Zelda character.

More *Mario Bros.*

Meanwhile, there was a huge demand in North America for a sequel to the *Super Mario Bros.* game. Because of this, Miyamoto modified an existing Japanese game called *Dream Factory: Doki Doki Panic,* so that it featured Mario, Luigi, and the princess. Nintendo released it as *Super Mario Bros. 2* in 1988.

The setting and characters in *Super Mario Bros. 3,* released in 1990, were similar to those in the original *Super Mario Bros.* It featured eight worlds, each containing numerous levels. In this game, King Bowser Koopa and his children have captured Princess Peach Toadstool and taken control of the Mushroom World. Players have to guide Mario as he tries to restore peace and rescue the princess.

Super Mario Bros. 3 introduced new gameplay elements. Magical suits gave Mario special abilities when he wore them. The Frog Suit enhanced his swimming and jumping skills, the Tanooki Suit gave him the power to turn into a statue, and the Sledgehammer Suit enabled him to throw hammers. He could also fly, when he wore a raccoon tail, and in certain levels he could find a warp whistle that had the power to whisk him away to a different world.

The game has a number of mysterious entrances with surprises that lie beyond them. Miyamoto says that in his travels he enjoys discovering things he had not expected to find. He wants to give players this same type of enjoyment, so he puts unexpected features like these in his games.

"When I was a child, I went hiking and found a lake," he says. "It was quite a surprise for me to stumble upon it. When I traveled around the country without a map, trying to find my way, stumbling on amazing things as I went, I realized how it felt to go on an adventure like this."[7]

A giant Super Mario statue stands out in a Nintendo display in Tokyo.

Super Mario World

When Nintendo first started planning to produce a Super Nintendo Entertainment System (SNES), Nintendo president Yamauchi wanted to offer people a good reason to buy it. Again, he asked Miyamoto to create a game that would show off the increased processing power of this new **video game console**.

In response, Miyamoto worked with a team of sixteen people, over a three-year period, to create *Super Mario World*. The new game was released in early 1991 along with the SNES. In this adventure Mario and Luigi travel to Dinosaur Island for a vacation. There they learn that King Bowser Koopa and his children have kidnapped the princess again and enslaved the kingdom. Mario sets off across the island's seven worlds and many levels to search for her.

Mario was given new skills in this game, and the game was also nonlinear—players could return to different worlds whenever

Two boys try out the Super Nintendo Entertainment System shortly after its release in 1991.

they wanted, instead of only moving forward. Even so, some critics claimed that this game was too similar to previous Mario games. Still, more than 20 million units were sold.

When asked how he creates internationally recognizable and deeply loved characters (such as Mario), Miyamoto says, "Making games 'fun' is our only objective, and we're always making an effort to accomplish this goal. I believe that the creation of game characters is simply one of the processes to achieve this goal. If *Mario* games hadn't been fun to play, the character wouldn't be popular at all."[8]

A New Console/A New Dimension

When Nintendo came out in 1997 with a new home console, the Nintendo 64, they released the *Super Mario 64* game with it. Until that year, Mario games had existed in only two dimensions. But, in this game, depth was added—Mario and his whole world became three dimensional, or 3D. By moving a 360-degree **analog stick**, which was located on the game's controller, players could make Mario run, walk, or jump in a totally new way. Miyamoto was enthusiastic about the Nintendo 64's powerful new graphic capabilities, saying, "Up to now, we have had trouble making games look as real as possible. But now these problems have been solved."[9]

In the game King Bowser Koopa has again kidnapped the princess and has stolen Power Stars that have long protected Mushroom Castle. He has hidden the stars inside the castle's paintings. Mario's challenge in this extremely popular game is to enter the paintings and recapture the stars.

The Legend of Zelda Sequels

Miyamoto believes it is important that a game be challenging for players. It must keep their interest high so that they become

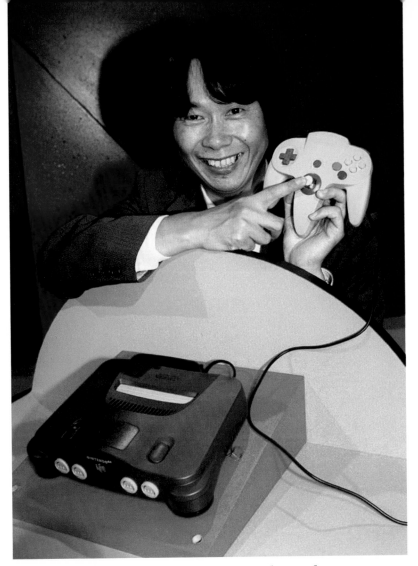

Miyamoto shows off his first 3D game player, the Nintendo 64 system.

deeply involved in the game play. For that to happen there must be intriguing action from the start, with numerous puzzles to solve. The hero should be forced to battle a worthy opponent, and they should be fighting over something of great worth, where a loss by the hero would be devastating.

After the strong sales of *The Legend of Zelda,* Miyamoto and his team produced a number of *Zelda* sequels, all of which did well. One of the most successful was the fifth game of the series, *The Legend of Zelda: Ocarina of Time*, which was released in 1998.

In this game, Link continues in his role as a hero trying to save Princess Zelda. His quest takes him through windswept deserts, over Death Mountain with its volcanic caves, and into eerie dungeons filled with murderous creatures. He is even forced

Nintendo introduces one of the many Zelda games, *The Legend of Zelda: Twilight Princess*, to the news media.

to travel back and forth through time, as he battles a powerful evil being. He will need both courage and wisdom to survive. If he fails, the land of Hyrule will fall into darkness and destruction.

Marriage and Family

Despite working long days as well as some nights on his best-selling games, Miyamoto found the time to meet a fellow Nintendo employee named Yasuko. After dating for a short while, they married.

Yasuko stopped working when the first of their two children was born. They bought a small house close enough to the Nintendo office for Miyamoto to walk or bicycle to work every day. Because of his work at Nintendo, Miyamoto does not have much free time, but when he does, he likes to swim, ski, and play his banjo. He especially likes American bluegrass music.

When Miyamoto walks about in Kyoto, fans sometimes wave and tell him they are great admirers of his work. Some call him Dr. Miyamoto, as a compliment to his high-quality work. Elsewhere, Miyamoto says he is rarely recognized, because he is just an average sort of guy.

CHAPTER 4

Game Master

Because of his knowledge and experience, Shigeru Miyamoto now oversees the development of many of Nintendo's biggest games. He works closely with current Nintendo president Satoru Iwata, choosing future projects for the company.

Miyamoto thinks that some video game companies make games that are not acceptable for children to play because of their violent content. He believes that great games can be suitable for all ages.

"I guess violence is one way you can elicit emotion and deliver entertainment to players. But at the same time I think it is more of an escape route for developers to use when they have a hard time coming up with ideas for creating fun,"[10] he says.

Nintendogs

One of Miyamoto's latest projects is a puppy simulator known as *Nintendogs*. It was released in the United States in August 2005, and made for the Nintendo dual-screen (DS), a handheld game player. At the start of this unique game, players must choose which version of the game to play: *Lab & Friends, Chihuahua & Friends,* or *Dachshund & Friends.* They then pick the puppy they want from a wide selection at a kennel. Players, who are also referred to as trainers in the game, can then bring their puppy home and do almost everything they would do if they were raising a real puppy, through the help of a **stylus,** a small pointed instrument, which comes with the DS.

Players communicate with their dog by speaking into the DS's microphone. The dog will respond to the sound of its owner's

An adorable, lifelike *Nintendog* puppy peers out of the Nintendo DS screen at two young players.

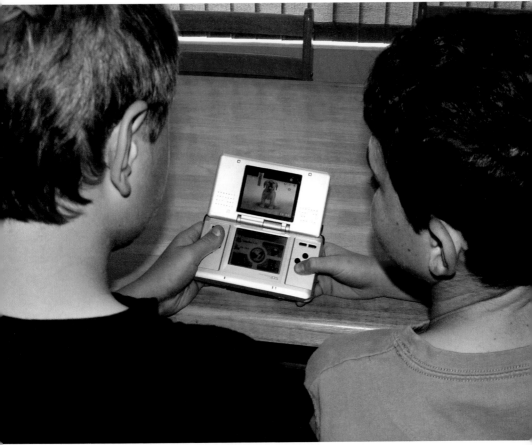

voice. Players can pet their dog by simply moving the stylus over the dog in a petting motion. Players can feed, water, and bathe their pet, too.

A Nintendog does many things that a real dog might do. For example, if a Nintendog passes another dog while on its way to the park, the two dogs will probably sniff each other a bit, and then each will go its own way.

The game's dog-training manual advises owners training a puppy to be clear, concise, and consistent when giving a command to a pet, similar to what one would do to train a real dog. Players can practice throwing a disc or tennis ball in the air and having their dog leap up to catch it. Eventually players can enter their dogs in competitions for disc catching, agility, and obedience. Winners earn trophies and money to pay for their dog supplies, or to buy another Nintendog.

Nintendogs has an unusual feature. If players keep their DS on the bark-mode setting and another *Nintendogs* player is within wireless range and on bark mode, the two players can make contact wirelessly, and the dogs can play together. "*Nintendogs* is so appealing to the masses because rather than trying to follow industry trends, it is based on things that people find appealing in general. Not just what they find appealing in video games,"[11] Miyamoto says.

Making a Video Game

What games to produce is an important decision for a company like Nintendo. It requires a long time to develop and test a game, and it can cost a million dollars, or more, to produce and promote the game through advertising. Also, the process of creating a game has changed dramatically since Miyamoto created *Donkey Kong* with only a handful of people. Now, artists, de-

Miyamoto promotes his *Nintendogs* game at a dog fashion show in New York.

signers, writers, and programmers, among others, are needed to do the work.

To make a game, Miyamoto meets with the top four people who will be involved in the project. They develop the basic concept and project plan. After the game's basic plan is completely mapped out, the design staff then gives detailed ideas to the programmers in the form of rough sketches and written instructions. Because it is a team effort, everyone on the team sits down and discusses different points about the game, sometimes late into the night.

Miyamoto says to make a game today he requires 20 to 30 people who will devote all their time to that project, and at least an additional 20 support people. The entire process of making a game can take up to three years. Generally, *Zelda* series games take longer than other games to produce, because of their complexity.

When a new game is being prepared, it has to be tested many times by different groups to make sure there are no problems and that the game is working the way it was designed to work. In addition to these tests, Miyamoto invites employees and their children to Nintendo to play a test version of the game, to see how much people like the game. At these tests he observes without saying anything, even when he would like to tell a player to do

Creating a new game can sometimes require the cooperation of more than 50 Nintendo employees.

The proud creator of so many Nintendo games shows off his Super Mario game, designed for the Nintendo DS.

something because it would help him or her later in the game. He watches to see if the children can handle the controls and how interested they are in the game.

Final Editing

When a game is almost ready, Miyamoto goes over its blueprint carefully. A blueprint describes the game's features, characters, story line, dialogue, puzzles, artwork, and other items. He examines the game's pathways, rooms, and puzzles, thinking through the moves a player might make to get to them. He looks for anything that needs to be changed. After almost thirty years of making games, he can tell if the game play is either too hard or too easy. He also looks to see if something can be added to the game to improve it, or to make it more fun to play.

When he has finished editing, the game goes back to the technicians, who work on the changes until Miyamoto is satisfied that the game is as good as he can make it. Finally, the music is composed and added, and the game is ready.

Because of the technological advances over the years, Nintendo, along with other video game companies, periodically develops new game-playing systems and games to go with them. While Miyamoto has been with Nintendo, the company has produced the Nintendo Entertainment System, the Super Nintendo Entertainment System, Game Boy, Nintendo 64, Game Boy Advance, GameCube, and the DS. Although Miyamoto has many years of experience developing games, there is always a new game-playing system for which to make games. This keeps him interested and inspired in his work.

When asked about his future plans, Miyamoto says, "A lot of film directors keep making movies until they die, so I think I'll keep making games for a long time."[12]

NOTES

Chapter 1: A Creative Mind

1. Quoted in Piaras Kelly, "Inside Nintendo: Shigeru Miyamoto," Gamers Europe, April 16, 2004. www.gamerseurope.com/articles/499.

2. Quoted in David Sheff, *Game Over*. New York: Random House, 1993, p. 46.

Chapter 2: Early Success

3. Quoted in a lecture and question-and-answer session given by Miyamoto, Tokyo University, July 3, 2003.

4. Quoted in Sheff, *Game Over,* p. 47.

5. Sheff, *Game Over,* pp. 49–50.

6. Quoted in Miyamoto Shrine: Shigeru Miyamoto's Home on the Web, "Miyamoto Interview," Mario Mania Players Guide, 1991. www.miyamotoshrine.com

Chapter 3: Nintendo's Shining Star

7. Quoted in Sheff, *Game Over,* p. 51.

8. Quoted in Marc Saltzman, *Game Creation and Careers: Insider Secrets from Industry Experts.* Indianapolis: New Riders, 2004, p. 172.

9. Quoted in David S. Jackson, "The Spielberg of Video Games," *Time,* May 20, 1996.

Chapter 4: Game Master

10. Quoted in Kris Pigna, ed., "Biography of Shigeru Miyamoto,"

Gamer-Talk.net, June 20, 2004. www.gamer-talk.net/feature 38.html.

11. Quoted in Chris Kohler, "The Man Who Keeps Nintendo Cool," Wired News: Joystick, June 15, 2005. www.wired. com./news/games/0,2101,67854.html.

12. Quoted in Kelly, "Inside Nintendo: Shigeru Miyamoto."

GLOSSARY

analog stick: A device used to move characters, normally intended to be used with the player's thumbs.

arcade games: Stand-alone game systems that are found in public places, such as video arcades, bowling alleys, amusement parks, and pizza parlors.

jump button: A button that players can push to make a character in a game jump into the air.

launch: To make a company's game or game system available for sale to the public for the first time.

pixels: Tiny dots that make up a picture in a computer's memory.

power-ups: Things that give a character in a game extra power or a special ability.

role-playing game (RPG): A game that involves the player in a journey of exploration and puzzle solving, and relies on character growth.

scrolled: Caused text or graphics to move up, down, or across the screen.

sequels: Games that are based on a previously released game.

stylus: A small, pointed instrument.

video game: A game played using an electronic device and displayed on a television set, computer monitor, or other viewing screen.

video game console: A dedicated electronic device designed to play video games.

For Further Exploration

Books

Cherie D. Abbey, ed., *Biography Today: Scientists & Inventors,* Vol. 5. Holmes, PA: Omnigraphics, 2001. This volume, which includes one chapter on Shigeru Miyamoto, features biographies of scientists and inventors who work in the computer and information-technology fields.

Arlene Erlbach, *Video Games.* Minneapolis: Lerner, 1995. This book tells how video games are made, and how game-playing systems work. It has an interesting section on how artists draw pictures with computers for games, and another section on how a video game's sound effects are produced.

Gloria Skurzynski, *Know the Score—Video Games in Your High-Tech World.* New York: Bradbury, 1994. This book tells how electronic games and programs are created. Readers learn where the ideas come from, who puts them together, and how they are developed into games.

Web Sites

Classic Gaming (www.classicgaming.com). This site contains information about many of the early *Mario* games, including *Mario Bros., Super Mario Bros., Super Mario Bros. 3, Super Mario World,* and others.

Miyamoto Shrine: Shigeru Miyamoto's Home on the Web (www. miyamotoshrine.com). This site has photographs of Miyamoto and information about the games he has created.

Nintendo (www.nintendo.com). Information is available at this site about Nintendo games, systems, codes, and strategies. News about any new games and/or game systems can be found here.

INDEX

Picture Credits

ABOUT THE AUTHOR

Jan Burns has written one other book for children, as well as many articles for newspapers and magazines. She holds a bachelor's degree in sociology from the University of California, Berkeley. She lives close to Houston, Texas, with her husband, Don, and sons, David and Matt.